Sally Knyvette in association with Theatre503
presents the world premiere of

BURNING BRIDGES

BY AMY SHINDLER

Burning Bridges was first performed at Theatre503, London,
on 13 September 2016

BURNING BRIDGES
BY AMY SHINDLER

CAST

Kate Thomas	Anne Adams
Sarah Seliman	Rae Brogan
Dan Thomas	Simon Bubb
Waitress	Gaby French
Policewoman	Rosemary Berkon
Policewoman/Waitress	Sarah Balfour
Policewoman	Abbie McCamley

CREATIVE TEAM

Director	Sally Knyvette
Designer	Max Dorey
Lighting Designer	Dan Saggars
Composer	Tim Phillips
Production Manager	Jon Armstrong
Deputy Stage Manager	Rike Berg
Producer	Trish Wadley
Assistant Producer	Sofia Broli
Graphic Designer	Mihaela Bodlovic

A Special Thank You to The Shirley Foundation, Autistica, Resources for Autism, Autism Eye, Aly Spiro from ALRA, and ALAG.

AUTHOR'S NOTE

When I came up with the idea for this play in early 2003, Asperger's syndrome was not in the mainstream consciousness in the way it is now, and was particularly under-diagnosed in women. My mother was a special educational needs teacher and so what I learned about AS came via the wonderful stories she told me about some of her students. I was always fascinated by their unusual, often brilliant, perspectives on life and the pride so many of them took in seeing the world differently from a 'Neuro Typical'.

The following year, my mum suffered two paralysing strokes and was diagnosed with terminal cancer. Communicating with her became heartbreakingly disengaged. With my life in a strange stasis, I found solace in beginning research for *Burning Bridges*. The months I spent in the British Library reading about AS connected me to my mum's life before her illness, bringing me closer to her and giving me hope in the brain's ability to cope and find peace through periods of severe stress.

When she died in February 2005, I threw myself into breathing life into my research and the characters that now appear on these pages. Life was chaotic at the time and was also raising questions about moral responsibility, loyalty and gender equality. So it's a dark piece that sprang from a dark year, but I hope that I have found compassion and humour too.

I really have to thank my mum for giving me the seed for this play and the impetus to sow it. There has also been a great deal of support and feedback from very smart and generous people along the way. So thank you also to my inspiring father, Colin Shindler, my talented frequent collaborator, Beth Chalmers, Amy Rosenthal, Ed Dyson, Bert Tyler Moore, Stephen Brown, Yasmin Wilde, Rivka Isaacson, Louiza Patikas, Harriet Pennington Legh, Tracy Wiles, Marie Phillips, Joel Reid, Dr Stephen M. Edelson of the Autism Research Institute, for sharing his knowledge and allowing me to use his writing to spin the plot, Sally Knyvette, who insisted I get this play out of a drawer a decade after I'd finished it, and Theatre503 for putting it on. Thank you also to the hundreds of AS, Autistic, and NT people who've written such wonderful, funny and eloquent blogs, books and articles – I so enjoyed sharing your world.

Amy Shindler

CAST AND CREATIVES

ANNE ADAMS (KATE THOMAS)
Chicago stage credits include: *The Old Masters* (Steppenwolf Garage Theater); *Cherry Orchard* (Steppenwolf); *Mauritius* (Northlight); *Orange Lemon Egg Canary* (Chopin); *This Is Our Youth, Life and Limb, Imagining Brad* (Pine Box).

Anne can be seen in the upcoming feature films *Samuel Street* directed by Aliakbar Campwala and *55 Steps* directed by Bille August. Also a writer, her play *Strange Country* was the inaugural recipient of New Light Theater Project's New Light New Voices Award and was produced in July 2016 in NYC.

RAE BROGAN (SARAH SELIMAN)
Rae's recent work includes: *Goosebumps Alive* (The Vaults); *Dick!* (Leicester Square) and *Call the Midwife* (BBC 1). Further credits include *Wannabes* (winner Best Comedy, Miami WebFest 2015); *NewsRevue* (Canal Café); *Stop Kiss* (Leicester Square); *DNA* (Courtyard). Rae is also currently developing *CSO: LDN*, a comedy script with writing partner Lucy Grainger.

SIMON BUBB (DAN THOMAS)
Simon trained at Webber Douglas. Theatre includes: *Saint Joan, War Horse, The Habit of Art, People* (National Theatre); *Much Ado About Nothing, Romeo and Juliet, King John* (RSC); *Much Ado About Nothing* (Shakespeare's Globe); *The Philanthropist* (Donmar Warehouse); *Noises Off* (Old Vic tour); *24 Hour Plays* (Old Vic New Voices); *Hay Fever* (Royal Exchange); *Far from the Madding Crowd* (Watermill); *The Importance of Being Earnest, Unless* (Stephen Joseph, Scarborough); *Stealing Sweets and Punching People* (Theatre503); *The Soft of Her Palm* (Finborough); *The Edge of the Land* (Eastern Angles).

Film includes: *Waiting for Dawn*. TV includes: *W1A, Red Dwarf, Father Brown, Holby City, EastEnders, Doctors*.

Radio includes: *The Archers, Expenses Only, Clare in the Community*, and dozens of radio plays as a member of the BBC Radio Drama Company.

AMY SHINDLER (PLAYWRIGHT)

Burning Bridges is Amy's first stage play. Amy began her career as an actress on TV, film and stage. Since 1999, she has played the role of Brenda Tucker on BBC Radio 4's *The Archers*.

Writing credits include: *Pat and Cabbage* (ITV); *Horrible Histories* (CBBC); *Trollied* (Sky 1); *Threesome* (Comedy Central); *My Family* (BBC 1); *Pauline Pepys' Dowry*, *Concrete Cow*, *The Sunday Format* (BBC Radio 4).

SALLY KNYVETTE (DIRECTOR)

Sally has been an actress in TV and theatre for many years and is best known for her leading roles as Jenna in *Blake's 7* and Kate in *Emmerdale*.

Her directing credits include: *Twelve Angry Men, Are you now or have you ever been?, Inherit the Wind, To Kill a Mocking Bird, Judgment at Nuremberg* (Tricycle); *A World Elsewhere* (Theatre503).

TIM PHILLIPS (COMPOSER)

Tim has worked widely in the music business since the Sixties, as composer, arranger, record producer, singer and session guitarist; his music has been used in films, television and commercials.

Theatre credits include: *Quiet Sun* (Oxford Playhouse); *Well Hell I Don't Know* (Edinburgh Fringe); *Sailing Down Everest* (Roundhouse, London*); Jack the Giant-Killer* (Hub, Cornwall); *Letters from Wyoming* (An Tobar, Isle of Mull); *Judgment at Nuremberg* (Tricycle).

MAX DOREY (SET DESIGNER)

Max graduated from the Professional Theatre Design MA at Bristol Old Vic Theatre School in 2012. He was a finalist for the Linbury Prize in 2013 and was a trainee/assistant designer at the RSC in 2013/14.

Set and costume design credits include: *Cargo* (Arcola); *Last of the Boys* (Southwark Playhouse); *After Independence* (Arcola/Papatango); *P'Yongyang* (Finborough); *No Villain* (Old Red Lion); *All the Little Lights* (Fifth Word); *And Then Come The Nightjars* (Theatre503/Bristol Old Vic); *Orson's Shadow*, *Teddy* (Southwark Playhouse); *Lardo, Marching on Together* (Old Red Lion); *Coolatully, Black Jesus* (Finborough); *Sleight and Hand* (Edinburgh Fringe); *I Can Hear You, This is Not an Exit* (The Other Place at the Courtyard, RSC/ Royal Court Upstairs); *Count Ory* (Blackheath Halls); *The Duke in Darkness*, *Marguerite* (Tabard); *Disco Pigs* (Bristol Old Vic Theatre School/Blue Crate); *The Good Soul of Szechuan, Macbeth* (Bristol Old Vic Theatre School); *Phaedra's Love* (Ravenrock/Holbeck/NSDF Scarborough).

DAN SAGGARS (LIGHTING DESIGNER)

Dan graduated from Technical Theatre Arts at Middlesex University. He designs many types of performance including theatre, opera and dance.

Design credits include: O&Co's *The Three Musketeers* (Kenton, Henley); *How to Win Against History* (Ovalhouse/Assembly's The Box, Edinburgh); *Alcina*, *Xerxes* (Longborough Festival Opera); *ECHO_NARCISSUS* (The Yard); *Bernarda Alba* (Cockpit); *The Lamellar Project* (South Hill Park Studio/UK touring for Alex Marshall Design); *Vanity Fair* (Middle Temple Hall); *Only Forever* (Hope); *Then Leap!* (The Lowry, Manchester).

TRISH WADLEY (PRODUCER)

Executive Producer of London theatre company Defibrillator.

Credits: Associate Producer on *My Night With Reg* (Apollo). For Defibrillator – Producer on *Insignificance* (Langham Place, New York), *The Armour* (Langham, London), *The Hotel Plays* (Langham, London & Grange Hotel), *The One Day of the Year*, *Hard Feelings* (Finborough).

She is a Director of The Uncertainty Principle, a theatre company established in both the UK and Australia.

Trish is a 2014 recipient of the Society of London Theatre (SOLT) Stage One Bursary for new theatre producers.

Theatre503 is the award-winning home of groundbreaking plays.

Led by Artistic Director Lisa Spirling, Theatre503 is a flagship new-writing venue committed to producing bold, brave new plays. We are the smallest theatre in the world to win an Olivier Award and we offer more opportunities to new writers than any other theatre in the UK.

THEATRE503 TEAM

Artistic Director	Lisa Spirling
Executive Director	Andrew Shepherd
Producer	Jessica Campbell
Literary Manager	Steve Harper
Literary Coordinators	Lauretta Barrow, Nika Obydzinski
Office Manager	Anna De Freitas
Resident Assistant Producers	Bridget Nesta, Audrey Thayer
Senior Readers	Kate Brower, Rob Young

THEATRE503 BOARD

Royce Bell, Peter Benson, Chris Campbell, Kay Ellen Consolver, Ben Hall, Dennis Kelly, Eleanor Lloyd, Marcus Markou, Geraldine Sharpe-Newton, Jack Tilbury, Erica Whyman (Chair), Roy Williams.

THEATRE503 HEROES

These brilliant volunteers give their valuable time and expertise to Theatre503 as front of house and box office managers, script readers and much more.

Alice Mason, Anna Middlemass, Anna Mors, Anna Landi, Andrei Vornicu, Asha Osborne, Annabel Pemberton, Bethany Doherty, Brett Westwell, Carla Grauls, Carla Kingham, Cecilia Garcia, Cecily King, Chelsey Gillard, Charlotte Mulliner, Chidi Chukwu, Damian Robertson, Danielle Wilson,D avid Benedictus, Dominic Jones, Elena Valentine, Emma Brand, Fabienne Gould, George Linfield, Gillian Greer, Imogen Robertson, Isla Coulter, James Hansen, Jim Mannering, Joanna Lallay, Joe Ackerman, Joel Ormsby, Kate Brower, Kelly Agredo, Ken Hawes, Larner Taylor, Lisa Cagnacci, Lucy Atkins, Maddy Ryle, Mandy Nicholls, Mark Doherty, Martin Edwards, Michelle Sewell, Mike McGarry, Nathalie Czarnecki, Nick Cheesman, Nicole Marie Bartlett, Paul Webb, Rahim Dhanji, Rebecca Latham, Reetu Sood, Rob Ellis, Saul Reid, Serafina Cusack, Sevan Greene, Simon Mander, Stephanie de Whalley, Stuart Quinn, Tamsin Irwin, Tess Hardy, Tim Bano, Tobias Chapple, Tom Hartwell, Tom Latter, Tommo Fowler, Valeria Bello, Valeria Montesano, Vanessa Garcia, Will Callaghan, Yasmeen Arden.

BURNING BRIDGES

Amy Shindler

In memory of Lynn

Characters

KATE THOMAS, *American, thirty-three*
DAN THOMAS, *English, thirty-nine*
SARAH SELIMAN, *American, has Asperger's syndrome,*
twenty-five
POLICEWOMAN
WAITRESS

The action takes place in the present.

This text went to press before the end of rehearsals and so may differ slightly from the play as performed.

Scene One

KATE *and* DAN's *flat – living room. Evening. It's in a modest but nicely decorated Victorian conversion in North-West London. The sofa's new, the floor is oak and there are some expensive rugs scattered about that suggest a fruitful holiday to Morocco or a familiarity with splurging on Etsy.*

The front door is unlocked and DAN *enters, carrying a suitcase. He's followed by* KATE *and then* SARAH, *who carries a backpack.* SARAH *is noticeably cautious about body contact, both with the others and with the space around her. She avoids eye contact most of the time, but when she does look at* KATE *or* DAN *she stares intensely.*

DAN *and* KATE *take their coats off.* SARAH *paces the room, looking around.* KATE *watches her, excitedly.*

KATE. So this is it! What do you think?

SARAH. It's small.

KATE. No.

SARAH. Teensy-weensy.

KATE. Actually for London this is pretty big.

> SARAH *scrutinises the wall, critically.*

SARAH. And you have a crack in the support wall indicating structural problems.

DAN. What?

> DAN *inspects the wall, worriedly.*

SARAH. Also it smells.

KATE. We've just repainted. We have pictures and stuff in storage. I just haven't gotten round to putting them up yet.

SARAH. You need them. Your wall colour sucks.

KATE. Right... Want something to drink?

SARAH. Mountain Dew.

KATE. We don't have that here. How about a Coke?

SARAH. What colour?

KATE. Silver.

SARAH. Yes.

DAN (*moving to the kitchen*). I'll get it.

> DAN *exits to the kitchen.* KATE *fishes a business card out of her purse.*

KATE. So I should probably call your friend from the plane.

SARAH. He was not my friend. He was an Asshole.

KATE. Still it would be a bummer for you to be deported before your vacation even begins. Just... hang out with Dan for a minute, okay?

> SARAH *sulks.* KATE *picks up her mobile and exits down the hall.*

> SARAH *looks for somewhere to put down her backpack and finds a patch of rug. She puts the bag down carefully, making sure it doesn't make contact with the floor. Then she surveys the sofa and the armchair, and decides to perch on the end of the sofa.*

> DAN *enters, holding two cans of Diet Coke. Seeing only* SARAH, *he looks a bit worried. He hands her a Coke.*

DAN. Sorry... did you want a glass... or...

SARAH. No.

> SARAH *turns the can of Coke around three times, blows on it, opens it and takes a slurp, still staring at him over the rim.*

DAN. I guess you must be quite jet lagged.

SARAH. No.

> *Pause.*

DAN. It's a long flight. Seven hours?

SARAH. Six hours, thirty-two minutes' flight time.

DAN. Right… you're good with numbers.

SARAH. I have a watch.

DAN. Time flies.

SARAH. What?

DAN. Nothing.

> SARAH *stares at* DAN, *unblinkingly. There's an awkward pause then:*
>
> (*Simultaneous*.) Kate said –

SARAH (*simultaneous*). Are you –

DAN. – sorry, ladies first.

SARAH. Why?

DAN. Why?

SARAH. Why ladies first?

DAN. I don't know. It's just something you're taught to say.

SARAH. I don't like being called 'a lady'.

DAN. What would you prefer to be called?

SARAH. Hot.

DAN (*beat*). So what were you going to ask… before?

SARAH. Did you Fall In Love with my sister at first sight?

DAN. Um… well, we met at work, so we were a bit… cautious.

SARAH. I see.

> *Pause.*

DAN. It's really nice to meet you finally. Sorry you couldn't make it to the wedding.

SARAH. That's okay. I didn't want to go.

DAN. Why?

SARAH. High probability you'd be an Asshole.

DAN. Right.

> *He laughs weakly.* SARAH *just stares at him.*

> (*Beat.*) So how's college?

SARAH. It's an integrated programme combining normal class curriculum with structured social and communication skills.

DAN. I meant do you enjoy it?

SARAH. So many questions. Jeez Louise!

DAN. Sorry.

SARAH. I want to ask you something.

DAN. Oh yeah sure… sorry.

SARAH. Did you Make Love with Kate on the first date?

> DAN *blinks.* KATE *enters.*

KATE. All straightened out. No charges. He was very understanding, considering. You would have to attack a retired cop.

SARAH. He said he was Jesus.

KATE. You know he didn't mean it li–

SARAH. I said, 'what's your name?' He said, 'Jesus' –

KATE. Come on –

SARAH. – he said –

KATE. – Sarah. Do you really think if Jesus turned up today – out of the blue – he'd be sitting next to you in Virgin Atlantic Economy?

DAN. It'd look a bit hypocritical if he went Business.

KATE. Not helping, Dan.

DAN. Right airline though.

SARAH. But that's just it: he was mendacious.

DAN. Mendacious?

SARAH. He lied. Do you want me to get you a dictionary? –

KATE. Sarah –

SARAH. – and he put his elbow on my armrest. And he made me cold with the fan.

KATE. Those aren't reasons to hit someone. (*Beat.*) So are you hungry? I could make pasta –

SARAH. I don't eat yellow. You used to know that.

KATE. Well, I have wholemeal linguine – so it's brown.

SARAH. Gross.

> SARAH *checks her digital watch.*

And I don't have dinner after six thirty.

KATE. I know – I just wasn't sure which time zone –

SARAH. I'd like a snack.

KATE. What kind of snack?

SARAH. Celery with peanut butter. Oreos on Sundays.

KATE. We've got celery.

SARAH. But on Special Days I only eat red.

KATE (*pleased*). Oh yes… And I'm guessing today's a Special Day!

SARAH. No.

DAN. So… I think the shop downstairs has peanut butter. I can nip down.

KATE. It's okay I'll go –

DAN. No, no, no. I'll do it.

KATE. Thanks.

DAN. Sure.

> DAN *hastily grabs his jacket and exits.* KATE *looks fondly at* SARAH, *who avoids eye contact.*

SARAH. Stop looking at me like that.

KATE. I can't help it. I'm... you know... excited!

SARAH. Why?

KATE. Because you're finally here! In London! Have you had any thoughts about what you'd like to do?

SARAH. Yes.

KATE. What?

SARAH. Watch all of *Babylon 5* from the beginning.

KATE. I don't know if that's on.

SARAH. That could be a Major Problem. You do have *Game of Thrones*, right?

KATE. I don't know –

SARAH. *Elementary*?

KATE. ...um –

SARAH. Well, this is going to be tedious.

KATE. We'll find it online or something. (*Beat.*) How's Reenie?

SARAH. Gone.

KATE. Gone where?

SARAH. She died.

KATE (*upset*). Sarah! That's terrible... How did she die?

SARAH. She just got sick and died.

KATE. Why didn't you tell me?

SARAH. You didn't ask.

   SARAH *gets out her laptop and starts to type, ignoring* KATE.

KATE. That's... my god. I didn't know.

SARAH. How could you, you didn't call for a month.

KATE. I'm so sorry... things have been a little crazy... have you been feeling sad, Sarah? It's okay to feel sad.

SARAH *is completely transfixed on the screen.*

Who took over from Reenie?

SARAH *keeps staring at the screen.*

Sarah? Someone has taken over from Reenie, right? Sarah?

SARAH. What?

KATE. Who took over? Who's your new Mentor?

SARAH *is absorbed in her laptop.*

You're graduating in two semesters. We need help getting you a job, finding a place to live.

SARAH *starts tapping away on her laptop.*

What are you doing?

KATE *comes round to look at the screen,* SARAH *slams the laptop shut. She reaches into her bag and pulls out a small box of chocolates.*

SARAH. This is for you. Congratulations On Your Promotion.

KATE. What promotion?

SARAH. When you came to see me at Thanksgiving, you said you were up for promotion.

KATE. Oh right… That didn't work out. There are some internal problems so…

SARAH. So no one got promoted?

KATE. No, someone got promoted. (*Beat.*) Dan actually.

SARAH. Dan?

KATE. Yes. It's great.

SARAH. I see. (*Beat.*) I guess we should save these for him then.

KATE. Oh he won't mind us making a dent.

KATE *opens the lid of the box.*

Looks like there's already a dent.

SARAH. Unfortunately I was forced to partially eat some of this gift due to inadequate airline food. (*Beat*.) Did Dan Fall In Love with you at first sight?

KATE. I don't know.

SARAH. But you love him?

KATE. Of course.

SARAH. Why?

KATE. Lots of reasons.

SARAH. Name three.

KATE. Sarah... I don't know.

SARAH. You can't think of any?

KATE (*sighs*). Okay. He's kind, he makes me laugh... he's got good values... morals or whatever.

SARAH. Would he sacrifice his life for others?

KATE. Why would he need to?

SARAH. In a hostage situation.

KATE. How am I supposed to answer that?

SARAH. Hmmm... You got married after only four hundred and fifty-seven days of dating him so I suppose it's unsurprising that you don't know.

KATE. Look the point is he's a good guy, okay?

SARAH. Even though he took your promotion?

KATE. He didn't *take* it. There were lots of applicants. I encouraged him to go for it.

SARAH. I see. So now he's your boss?

KATE. No. He's working with another team. We can fill each other in on different projects this way. It's good, Sarah.

SARAH. Good for now.

KATE. What about you anyway? What happened to that guy with the fez? The one who came to Reenie's Thanksgiving last year?

SARAH *starts to open the laptop,* KATE *closes it.*

What was his name…

SARAH. Jeremy. He made me mad. We argued.

KATE. What about?

SARAH. Whether he had cystitis.

DAN *enters through the front door with a bag.*

DAN. Didn't know what you prefer, Sarah, crunchy or smooth, so I got both.

SARAH. Crunchy tastes like vomit.

DAN. Okay.

SARAH. Can I take a shower please?

KATE. Sure, I'll show you how the bathroom works.

SARAH. Do you have a jacuzzi function?

KATE. No, Sarah, this isn't *The Kardashians.* The shower's in the bath.

SARAH. Ewww. Gross.

KATE. It's the door on the left –

SARAH. I'll find it –

SARAH *leaves.*

DAN (*worried*). Is she okay?

KATE. She's fine. Better than I expected actually – considering she's out of her routine.

DAN. I don't think she approves of us getting married.

KATE. She doesn't approve of anything I do. She's still mad at me.

DAN. For what?

KATE. Everything.

DAN. Has she always been like that?

KATE. No… Not when she was really little. She was obsessed with me then. If I didn't play with her or sit next to her, she'd scream her head off. And then one day she replaced me with an empty Captain Crunch cereal box. Just like that. That's Sarah for you. Brutal.

DAN pulls her on to the sofa next to him and puts his arm around her.

Sometimes I feel like I've spent my whole life waiting for that connection again. Which makes me basically a total idiot.

DAN. You're my favourite idiot.

She leans into him as he strokes her hair. Suddenly, there's an electronic beep from somewhere nearby.

KATE. Is that me?

She picks up her handbag and starts rifling through it.

DAN. Leave it.

KATE. I should check it's not work.

DAN. You took holiday. Don't let Axley bully you.

KATE. It's fine. I know how to deal with him…

She pulls her phone out and checks it.

Wait… No… It's not me.

There's another beep. DAN runs his hand between the sofa cushions, looking for the source of the sound.

DAN. It's coming from here.

SARAH comes in, wearing tracksuit bottoms and a T-shirt. She hears the beeping and races towards DAN.

SARAH (*panicked*). You're sitting on Harry Styles!

DAN. What?

SARAH. My Tamagotchi Friend! He fell out! Stand up! Stand up!

DAN *jumps to his feet, alarmed.* SARAH *digs around in the sofa,* KATE *goes to help her.* KATE *finds the Tamagotchi – a small, plastic, computerised toy – down the back of the sofa.*

KATE. Hey, we used to have these as kids, didn't we?

SARAH *grabs the Tamagotchi out of her hands.*

SARAH. Don't touch him!

KATE. Why not?

SARAH. You might kill him.

KATE. I'm not going to kill him.

SARAH. You might press a button and feed him, or give him medicine by mistake.

KATE. Okay. Fine. I'll just look, okay?

SARAH *pushes a button to stop the noise and then holds it up for* KATE *to look at.*

Oh yes. I remember these… How sweet, he's a baby.

SARAH (*scathing*). He's a Duck.

KATE. Oh.

SARAH. He's been alive for eighty-eight generations. When he gets past ninety-nine, he'll beat all the records and then I'm going to tweet One Direction, and when they next tour they might invite me up on stage to give me an award. I might even sing a song with them.

DAN. How do you know what the record is?

SARAH. Message boards.

DAN. But how do you know it's true?

SARAH. Are you calling me a liar?

DAN. No.

SARAH. It's impossible for me to lie.

DAN. Really?

SARAH. You think I'm lying about not lying? –

KATE. Sarah –

SARAH. It's part of my diagnosis. (*To* KATE.) Can we go to the movies?

KATE. Whatever you want, sweetheart. It's so great to have you here – two weeks isn't long enough!

SARAH. Really?

KATE. No. You'll have to come back for summer vacation.

SARAH (*pointedly*). Dan wouldn't want me to stay that long.

DAN. No, no, it's… great that you're here. Really. We might just have to hold Harry Styles hostage to keep you here.

SARAH *takes this in for a second and then laughs a real belly laugh.* DAN *and* KATE *join in, surprised.*

SARAH. That's funny. You're really funny!

DAN. Thanks.

SARAH. Well, I have some Terrific News.

KATE. What's that?

SARAH. I *am* going to stay here.

KATE *freezes.*

KATE. What do you mean?

SARAH. I'm not going home!

KATE. You have school, Sarah –

SARAH. I can't go there any more. Can't afford it.

KATE. What? What happened to your fund?

SARAH. I lost it.

KATE. How?!

SARAH. Online poker.

KATE *and* DAN *stare at her in complete shock.*

KATE. What?

SARAH (*in a computer voice*). Game over. You lose.

End of Scene One.

Scene Two

Living room. Two weeks later. The apartment is very neat. On the table sits a plate of biscuits. KATE is erratically dusting – driven more by panic than perfectionism. SARAH enters and watches her from the doorway for a few moments. Then she goes into the kitchen and comes out with a duster. She begins to follow KATE around the room, polishing where she's just been polishing. After a beat, KATE clocks her.

KATE. What are you doing?

SARAH. You keep missing spots.

KATE. Have you read it yet?

SARAH. No.

KATE. She's going to be here any minute!

SARAH. They're all boring.

KATE. There are over two hundred courses.

SARAH. I know. Somebody should get fired.

KATE. Sarah, please. Work with me.

Annoyed, SARAH slopes off down the hall to her room.

KATE surveys the room and disappears into the kitchen. DAN enters through the front door. He takes off his coat and chucks it on the sofa.

DAN (*calling*). Hi.

KATE (*off*). Crap.

KATE enters.

DAN. Hello.

She picks up her purse from the side table.

KATE. We're out of milk. For tea.

DAN. So we can just drink it black.

KATE. We have to offer it. We need to come across as, you know… on top of stuff.

DAN. She said it's just an informal chat.

KATE. That's code for interview.

DAN. You really think the clincher will be milk?

KATE. She's doing us a huge favour, coming here…

DAN. Okay. I'll go to the shop.

KATE. No, I'll go. Just tell Sarah she'd better have a course chosen by the time I get back.

KATE *starts to go.*

DAN. Hey…

KATE *looks at him questioningly. He comes over and kisses her.*

It's going to be fine, okay? We've got this.

KATE (*gratefully*). Yeah. Thanks. (*Going.*) Don't eat the cookies!

KATE *exits.* DAN *goes into the kitchen.*

SARAH *enters from the hall. She scans the room – notices* DAN*'s coat on the sofa. She scurries back down the hall. After a beat we hear the shower running.*

DAN *enters from the kitchen, checking his phone. He looks at the plate of biscuits – hesitates… then takes one, shifting the arrangement to cover up the theft.*

The shower is turned off and after a bit, SARAH *enters. She's wrapped in a towel and combing her wet hair. She regards* DAN *for a moment; he hasn't noticed her yet.*

SARAH. Hello.

DAN *starts.*

DAN. Hi.

SARAH. I've had a shower.

DAN. Oh. Yeah. (*Beat*.) Kate's gone for milk. She said you
should pick a course.

SARAH. She's bossy.

DAN. Well, you know…

SARAH. No.

Under the following, SARAH *starts to carefully tiptoe
around the room, when she gets to the edge of a rug, she
hesitates, then jumps to the next one. She seems completely
absorbed in this game.* DAN *watches her, bemused.*

Which course do you think I should do?

DAN. Um… what are your interests?

SARAH. TV, One Direction, Bears, Gandhi, Oral Sex… But not
in that order.

DAN (*beat*). Right. Maybe you could do something media
focused. Or computer sciences?

SARAH. Which is better?

DAN. Whatever you're more interested in. Technology
produces the billionaires.

SARAH. I'd like to be a detective. Like Sherlock Holmes.

DAN. I'm guessing that's not a course.

SARAH. No. But I'm very good at noticing things. (*Smiles,
coquettishly.*) *Mr Thief.*

DAN. What?

She stops and points at the plate of biscuits.

SARAH. There were eleven and now there's ten.

DAN. Wow. You're good.

SARAH. Kate said we weren't allowed.

DAN. Yeah, no, I know. But she's not as observant as you.

SARAH. No she's not!

DAN. So let's not tell her, okay?

SARAH *smiles, pleased. She starts combing her hair again.*

SARAH. Okay… It'll be Our Little Secret.

The comb gets stuck in a tangle.

Ow.

She fights to get the comb out of her hair with one hand and holds on to the towel with the other, but the tangle gets increasingly worse as she chops at it.

OW!

DAN *watches her uncomfortably for a beat and then gets up to help her.*

DAN. Here let me –

SARAH. It's stuck –

DAN. – let go a minute –

SARAH *yields up the comb and* DAN *painstakingly untangles it from her hair. Although they don't touch,* SARAH *is acutely aware of* DAN*'s proximity and her vulnerable state but, unusually, she doesn't recoil.*

DAN *releases the comb and hands it to her.*

There you are.

SARAH. Thank you.

The front door opens and KATE *enters, looking stressed.* DAN *instinctively moves away from* SARAH *and sits back on the sofa.*

KATE. Got all the way down there before I realised I had no cash! Sarah, where are your clothes?

SARAH. I just took a shower.

KATE. Why? You took one an hour ago. Get dressed, come on!

SARAH stomps off to her bedroom and slams the door.
SARAH's Tamagotchi starts to beep persistently.

What's that now?

DAN. Is it her duck thing?

DAN drops to his hands and knees and has a look under the sofa.

It's coming from here.

KATE gets down beside him.

KATE. I don't see it… Wait, no, it's in here somewhere.

KATE begins pulling the cushions off the sofa. DAN joins her. She finds the Tamagotchi under the cushions. Its beeping has escalated to a shrill buzz.

(*Calling.*) Sarah!… How do you make it stop?

The doorbell buzzes.

She's here – perfect.

DAN. I'll go down and let her in. See if you can shut it up.

KATE throws the cushions back on the sofa. She shouts down the hall.

KATE. Sarah! She's here!

The Tamagotchi is still shrieking, she pokes at the buttons as DAN goes to open the front door.

SARAH enters, now dressed, just as KATE gets the Tamagotchi to stop. She rushes over and grabs it out of her hands, staring at it in horror.

SARAH. NO!!!

End of Scene Two.

Scene Three

Living room. Twenty minutes later. DAN *is looking out of the window into the communal gardens. The room is a mess; the plate is upside down on the floor; biscuits scattered around it.* KATE *kneels on the floor, picking up the detritus.*

KATE. How's she doing down there?

DAN. She's by the pond. I'm not entirely sure but… could she be administering last rites?

KATE. Probably. (*Beat.*) I feel awful.

DAN. You didn't do it on purpose.

KATE. She said I killed her only friend.

DAN. She'll get over it.

KATE. And now she'll never get to release a song with One Direction or whatever.

DAN. Surely that's a win win for everyone.

KATE. So what do we do about…?

DAN. We ask for another meeting.

KATE. After Sarah threw a plate at her?

DAN. There must be other places, courses.

KATE. Mid-semester? For students with special needs?

DAN (*beat*). Have you heard from the lawyer?

KATE. Not since last week.

DAN. But she's good?

KATE. Good at issuing invoices. (*Beat.*) Apparently Sarah's access to the money should have been monitored by the trustee of her fund.

DAN. Who's that?

KATE. Me.

DAN. Fuck.

KATE. Yeah.

DAN. There's got to be someone else… just till this gets sorted out. Your dad?

KATE. You're kidding, right?

DAN. People change.

KATE. You want me to ask that alcoholic, cowardly shit for help?

DAN. I'm just saying –

KATE. She hates him. I hate him. He didn't even turn up to Mom's funeral!

DAN. Okay. But won't Sarah go mental – shit, sorry, I mean… we can't leave her by herself all week, can we? What if she starts gambling again?

KATE. We could put a block on the internet – restrict access…

DAN. How will that go down?

KATE *looks grim.*

Maybe you should ask for more time off.

KATE. I may as well resign.

DAN. Just ask.

KATE. We're right in the middle of IGP 2. I can't just abandon everyone. And Axley's coming in next week.

DAN. He'll understand.

KATE. No, he won't.

DAN. Let me talk to him.

KATE. No.

DAN. He's okay, you know. He'll get it.

KATE. Dan, no. Don't get involved.

DAN. You know you're underestimating yourself. He needs you. The team needs you.

KATE. Really?

He goes over to her and holds her.

DAN. Axley called it after your interview. He said we'd better raise our game cos you made us look like a bunch of muppets. (*Affectionately.*) And you were the only woman he'd ever met who made safety goggles look hot.

KATE *pulls away.*

KATE. So he hired me because he thought I was hot.

DAN. What? No.

KATE. That's what you just said.

DAN. It was a compliment! Come on, you're attractive… you're working with a bunch of ugly blokes. You're going to get noticed.

KATE. I want to be noticed for my work!

DAN. You are. That's why he told us to raise our game.

KATE (*beat; quietly*). Is that why I didn't get the job? Because he doesn't take me seriously? –

DAN. What? –

KATE. – because I mean between the two of us I was the more qualified.

DAN. What? No. I mean… I don't know why… I suppose it could have been a… personality thing –

KATE. Meaning?

DAN. Meaning maybe he felt more comfortable with me. I mean… it's possible.

KATE. So I did lose out to you because I'm female?

DAN (*annoyed*). Or I dunno, maybe he actually thinks I'm good at my job. Jesus!

Pause.

KATE *goes over to the window.*

KATE. Melting plastic into the carp pond… the garden committee's going to love that.

DAN *joins her at the window.*

DAN. Is that a pyre…?

KATE. Yep.

Pause.

It's all been kinda crappy lately, hasn't it? What shall we do for your birthday?

DAN. It's not for two months.

KATE. It'll give us something to look forward to.

DAN. We could go back to that hotel in Shrewsbury?

KATE. Where?

DAN. You know the one – when we snuck away from the conference. When everything was all secret.

KATE. The one with the shouty woman with the glasses?

DAN. That wasn't my overriding memory, but, yes.

KATE. Didn't her dog try to rape you?

DAN. Yes, clearly we took away very different moments… I just remember it being a romantic hotel with a hot tub.

KATE. It was gorgeous.

DAN. Do you fancy it? You. me. Champagne. The jacuzzi…

KATE. The sinister shadow of a basset hound trying to heave himself over the side.

They laugh.

It's such a nice idea and I mean I'd love to…

DAN.…but?

KATE. I was just thinking more dinner or something. We can't really leave Sarah.

DAN (*resigned*). Right.

KATE. Hey…

She leans into him and kisses him. DAN *breaks away after a moment and looks out the window.*

DAN. Harry Styles is still on fire. I reckon we've got a good twenty minutes...

He kisses her more emphatically. After a moment she gently pushes him back.

KATE. I should go see if she's okay.

She pulls on a jacket and starts to leave.

DAN (*lightly*). You know, I like your sister, but she's killed the element of spontaneous sex in our marriage.

KATE (*lightly; leaving*). Did we have spontaneous sex in our marriage?

DAN. I did.

They grin at each other, but it feels strained.

End of Scene Three.

Scene Four

The living room. Evening. Two months later. KATE is lying on the sofa, eyes closed. She looks different to before: unwashed hair, tracksuit bottoms. Around her the room is in disarray. Mugs and half-drunk water glasses crowd the table, a heap of laundry has been dumped on a chair, a bowl of congealed porridge sits on the bookshelf.

The front door opens, DAN comes in.

DAN. Hey!

KATE. Hi.

KATE opens her eyes but doesn't bother sitting up. She seems different: drained of energy, apathetic.

DAN. Sorry I'm late. I was halfway out the door and Axley dragged me to the pub.

KATE. It's fine.

DAN. He's been approached to present a Radio 4 show, the jammy bastard. I suggested calling it *Bac Teria the Future*.

He grins at KATE, *hoping for an appreciative snigger, but she doesn't look at him.*

Where's Sarah?

KATE. Her room probably.

DAN. Have you eaten?

KATE. She had cereal or something.

DAN. What have you had?

KATE. Nothing.

DAN. I could get takeaway?

KATE. I'm not hungry.

DAN. Hey, I booked a restaurant for tomorrow. I think you'll like it… It's Japanese – Mexican fusion. The home of the 'Sushito'. Which is a sushi burrito apparently… Actually it sounds disgusting. But you know… it looks fun. Which we could do with.

KATE *just closes her eyes.* DAN *sighs and goes into the kitchen where he clatters around. The sound of crashing pots and pans is grating and we see* KATE *getting increasingly tense with each resounding bang.*

KATE. Dan… Dan…

Unable to stand it any more, she yells.

What the hell are you doing in there?

DAN *reappears.*

DAN. I'm going to scramble some eggs.

KATE. I already told you, I'm not hungry.

DAN. It's for me if that's all right. What the hell's wrong with you?

KATE. Nothing. (*Beat.*) I left you a message. You didn't call me back.

DAN (*unapologetic*). Right. Sorry. I was in meetings all day. What did you want to chat about?

KATE. I got fired.

DAN. What?!

KATE (*bitterly*). Axley *axed* me. He didn't tell you?

DAN. What? No!... Why?

KATE. The deadline's been brought forward. He needed someone who could work 'more competitive hours'.

DAN. I don't fucking believe it!

KATE. He's right. They can't afford to carry me just because my life's up shit creek.

DAN. Oh, darling.

He goes over to give her a hug, but she's stiff and he lets go quickly.

They'll have to pay you off.

KATE. Yeah.

DAN. We'll find you something else – let me ask around.

KATE. Sure, it'll be easy. I'll be like, hi, here's my CV, oh and by the way, I can only work three days a week and I may have to rush home at a moment's notice if my sister locks herself out or sets fire to the kitchen – which she does every other week.

Pause.

DAN. You know, we could look at this another way. As the beginning of something.

KATE. What?

DAN. Well, maybe it's time to... you know... start a family.

KATE. Are you serious?

DAN. Yeah.

KATE (*beat*). No.

DAN. What do you mean, 'no'?

KATE. I mean, no, I don't want kids.

DAN. Since when?

KATE. Since we got Sarah. (*Beat.*) And you know what the past three months have taught me? I'm an awful parent. I'm totally missing the maternal gene.

DAN. And that's it?

KATE *shrugs*.

Are you worried about having an autistic child?

KATE. Jesus.

DAN. I understand you're upset.… but you can't just drop that one on me like there's no room for discussion.

KATE. You know what? I've just been fired. So I'm finding it a bit hard to give a fuck about having a discussion.

DAN. Look, let's just… I think things will look very different once you get a bit of perspective. You might see the positive –

KATE. I'm sorry, 'the positive'?

DAN. I just think if we do want kids –

KATE. Did you not just –

DAN. Yeah I get it. You've changed your mind. Not very fair on me though, is it?

KATE. It wasn't very fair of you to convince me to commit professional suicide.

DAN. Wait a minute, this isn't my fault. I was thinking about what was best for Sarah!

KATE. You were thinking about what was best for you. Because apparently it's high time I quit prancing about in a lab coat and start making babies.

DAN. Don't put words in my mouth.

KATE. But that's right, isn't it?

DAN (*quietly*). I'm nearly forty. I want a family.

KATE. You used to say you were attracted to me because of my drive, my independence… but that wasn't what really turned you on, was it? What you were really after was the challenge of getting me to fit in with *your* plans –

DAN. Don't exaggerate –

KATE. – and apparently you assumed, when the time was right for you, that I'd kiss my career goodbye and play stay-at-home mom and wife.

DAN. I should be so lucky.

KATE. Excuse me?

DAN. It seems to me that 'playing wife' might involve some kind of physical contact with your husband.

KATE. Don't hijack this.

DAN. Why not? You've laid out your grievances – here's mine.

KATE. We have sex.

DAN. We don't.

KATE. We did it Saturday.

DAN. No. I did it Saturday. You lay there glaring at me like I'd clamped your car.

KATE. I was doing you a favour.

DAN. Thanks. Is it the act itself or just me that you're suddenly averse to?

KATE. Does it matter?

DAN. Only in the sense of trying to save our marriage.

KATE. Don't be such a drama queen.

DAN. You think I'm being dramatic do you? We've stopped talking, our sex life's gone to shit, you don't seem to particularly like me – everything we had before Sarah arrived feels… annihilated.

KATE. It's not Sarah's fault. She didn't ask me to sacrifice my job, you did.

DAN. So I'm to blame for everything, am I? You had no part in the decision?

KATE *gets up and starts putting on her coat.*

Kate, please. Talk to me.

KATE. I have to go.

DAN. Where?

KATE. Out.

DAN. What do I do about Sarah?

She looks at him impassively.

KATE. She'll need a new toothbrush, she won't reuse the same one more than twice. And she'll want a fresh towel every time she showers which is about four times a night. Don't try to give her the same one, even if it's dry, she'll notice. If she can't sleep she'll want to watch *Babylon 5*. We're currently on episode one hundred and two, series five: *Meditations on the Abyss*. Or she may want to play her CDs, she likes One Direction, Kanye West and for some reason 'Greensleeves' on the pipe organ. If she starts to freak out, I suggest earplugs and vodka. For you, not her.

KATE *exits, slamming the front door behind her.*

End of Scene Four.

Scene Five

The following evening. The living room has been vigorously tidied. SARAH *is staring intently at herself in the mirror, nervously trying to style her hair. She clearly has no idea what to do and gives up, annoyed. She picks up a lipstick, investigating it carefully. Then she scrutinises her face, critically, but can't quite bring herself to apply the lipstick. The lock turns in the front door – she gives a brief scream of excitement, and then quickly scampers back down the hall and into her room.*

DAN *slams through the front door and chucks his keys on the table.*

DAN. Kate?

> DAN *exits into the hall.*

> (*Off.*) Kate?

He storms back into the living room, pulls his mobile out of his coat pocket, checks it and shoves it back in his pocket. He exits into the kitchen.

> (*Off.*) Fuck's sake!

DAN *re-enters the living room, screwing up a Post-it note. He goes out through the hall door for a minute.*

> (*Off.*) Sarah?

He re-enters the living room, takes out his mobile and dials KATE's *number. It goes to answerphone. He chucks the Post-it on the floor.*

SARAH *enters, standing just inside the doorway.* DAN *doesn't notice her.*

> (*Into phone.*) Happy fucking birthday to me, eh? Well, fuck you too!

He bangs the phone down.

SARAH. Hello.

> DAN *starts.*

DAN. Christ, Sarah. I was just… Have you seen Kate?

SARAH. Yes.

DAN. When?

SARAH. She came in at 2.39 p.m.

DAN. What did she say?

SARAH. She said, 'Sorry I wasn't here when you woke up. Dan and I had a fight and I need space to think. Don't worry it's not your fault. Have you eaten?'

DAN. And then what happened?

SARAH. I ate a carrot.

DAN. No – where did she go?

SARAH. She went to Jen's.

DAN. Did she say when she'd be back?

SARAH. No. She took a bag and some underwear and some make-up remover and some deodorant and her toothbrush. But not toothpaste, so that could be a Major Problem.

DAN. Did she say anything else?

SARAH. She said sorry... She said she left you a note.

DAN. She did.

SARAH. What did it say?

DAN. 'Sorry'.

SARAH. Do you want me to sit on your chest?

DAN. What?

SARAH. It feels nice. It stops the fizzing. Shall I?

DAN. No, no. Thanks.

SARAH. Well, can you sit down? You're making me feel weird.

DAN *hesitates and then sits*.

Thanks. Wait there –

SARAH *scampers excitedly towards the kitchen*.

DAN. She's just so angry with everything. With me.

SARAH stops in the doorway, unsure whether she should keep going to the kitchen. She hovers nervously under the following.

And it's not my fault. That's the irony here! *I'm* the one on her side! But she won't… (*Beat.*) Has she said anything to you?

SARAH looks confused. DAN tries to hide his exasperation.

About us.

SARAH. Oh. (*Thinks; then.*) I don't think she loves you.

DAN (*reeling*). She said that?

SARAH (*brightly*). No, I can just tell. There was this guy when she was at college, she used to bring him to visit. She really loved *him*. (*Chirpily.*) Stay right there, I'll be Two Ticks…

SARAH skips into the kitchen. DAN looks like he's going to be sick. He puts his head in his hands for a moment and then looks at his phone. He's about to type a message but changes his mind.

Quietly, SARAH pops out of the kitchen and turns the lights down. DAN looks up, confused.

DAN. Sarah?

SARAH comes in, wearing a party hat and carrying a cake with candles. It's a very wonky, home-made cake.

SARAH (*singing, loudly*).
Happy Birthday to you,
Happy Birthday to you,
Happy Birthday dear Daaaaaaa-aaaan,
Happy Birthday to you!

She puts the cake down on the table in front of him. He just stares at it.

(*Beat.*) You have to blow out the candles.

DAN blows them out. SARAH cheers and jumps up and down.

(*Proudly.*) I knew it was your birthday so I made this. It's
a chocolate cake. I normally use Miracle Whip but they don't
have that here so I used mayonnaise which is basically the
same thing.

DAN. Okay.

SARAH. You just have to really go at it with a fork. My...
friend, Reenie, used to say 'Don't Be Afraid To Take
Whisks'. (*Laughs.*) *Whisks*, get it?

She laughs again, even harder. DAN *just watches her.*

DAN. Can you put the lights back up please?

SARAH (*generously*). It's *your* birthday.

She goes back to the wall and turns the lights up.

So I've thrown you a party – now it's time for a game...
I'm game if you are!

She laughs again and then looks at him expectantly.

I feel like you're not understanding my jokes.

DAN. Sorry, look I need to... go.

DAN *gets up.*

SARAH. Go where? What are you going to do?

DAN. I don't know... Get shit-faced.

He starts to head towards the door.

SARAH. If Kate comes back here should I tell her you've gone
to Get Shit-Faced then?

DAN *pauses.*

Just wait here.

SARAH *goes into the kitchen and comes back with a bottle
of vodka and two shot glasses. She goes to a bureau and gets
out the Genus Edition of Trivial Pursuit.*

She starts to set up the board. DAN *watches her.*

DAN. Look, I'm not –

SARAH. I'm always green, what do you want to be?

DAN. Sarah –

SARAH. Pink then. Here – roll.

She offers him the die. After a second, he reluctantly crosses to the table and rolls but doesn't sit down.

Five. Let's play Ibble Dibble.

DAN. What?

SARAH. You have to say Ibble Dibble and drink a shot every time you get an answer wrong. If you don't say Ibble Dibble, you have to drink two.

DAN. A drinking game? Are you supposed to –

SARAH. You said you wanted to Get Shit-Faced. Please move your pie.

DAN *reluctantly sits and moves his pie.*

You have chosen Sport.

She reads from a question card. Note: reading isn't easy for her.

Who in 1985 became the youngest male singles… champion at… Wimbledon?

DAN. Boris Becker?

SARAH. Yes! Roll again.

DAN *rolls and checks out his options.*

DAN. Science.

SARAH. You can't have Science. You can have History or Geography.

DAN (*wearily*). Fine. History.

SARAH (*reading*). Which US President preceded Theodore Roosevelt?

DAN. I don't know. Sarah… I can't think about this right now.

SARAH (*reading*). President William H. Taft. You have to drink.

DAN. I didn't give you an answer.

SARAH. Were you going to say President William H. Taft?

DAN. No.

SARAH. Drink.

> SARAH *pours him a shot of vodka. He hesitates for a moment and then downs it.*

> (*Excitedly.*) You didn't say Ibble Dibble! You have to drink again!

DAN. Sarah.

> SARAH *fills the glass again.*

> Fuck it.

> DAN *downs it instantly this time.*

SARAH. My go.

> *She rolls and moves.*

DAN (*reading; distractedly*). Right... um... Geography... What is the deepest known area on the earth?

SARAH. The Mariana Trench.

> DAN *checks the back of the card.*

DAN. That is... impressively correct.

> SARAH *rolls the die – and moves on to a wedge square.*

> And a very jammy roll. Okay for a wedge... This is a difficult one... What is the density of water?

SARAH (*thinks*). One gram per millilitre.

DAN (*checking the card*). Wow.

> *He hands her a wedge.*

> So you're pretty smart.

SARAH. I just remember things.

DAN. Are you good at maths? What's... sixty-three million four hundred and ninety-eight thousand divided by thirteen?

SARAH. Why do you expect me to know that?

DAN. I just thought you – you're…

She begins to tug a strand of hair with her hand.

SARAH. I'm not Rain Man.

DAN. No, no – I didn't mean to be – sorry.

SARAH. Do you know what an idiot savant is?

DAN. Yes.

SARAH. Because I'm not one of them.

DAN. No.

SARAH. I can't read two pages at the same time or construct the Eiffel Tower out of matchsticks.

DAN. I didn't mean – I…

SARAH. People are different –

DAN. Yeah. Sorry.

Pause.

DAN *reaches out and gently releases* SARAH*'s hand from the hair pulling. She goes rigid with fright momentarily and they're locked in a mid-air arm-wrestle, but then she slowly lets him lower it. He removes his hand from hers and she stares at where he touched her. She starts babbling.*

SARAH. You smell nice.

DAN. Thanks.

SARAH. Sometimes smells hurt. Like glasses when they come out of the dishwasher. But you smell good, like a forest when it's fall and the leaves go crunchy red, and the earth is all soft and smoky and you want to snuggle down into it like a mole and sleep.

DAN. I think it's just Head & Shoulders.

SARAH. I had a boyfriend. Did Kate tell you?

DAN. No.

SARAH. We broke up though.

DAN. Oh. Sorry.

SARAH. I loved him but he said I texted too much. So I pointed out his bladder problem.

DAN. Ah.

SARAH. It's okay I'm over it now. I set fire to his hat.

> DAN *tries hard not to laugh, but can't help it. After a moment,* SARAH *joins in.*

DAN. Shall we carry on?

> SARAH *rolls the die and moves.*

Sport. Okay. Which boxer famously won the 1974 'rumble' in Zaire?

SARAH (*downcast; mumbling*). I don't know.

DAN. Really? It was Muhammad Ali.

SARAH. See, I'm not a genius.

DAN. Far from it.

> SARAH *looks offended, but then* DAN *smiles and* SARAH *smiles back. She pours herself a vodka shot, turns it around three times and blows on it.*

SARAH. Down The Hatch!

> *She drinks. Then gasps.*

I didn't say Ibble Dibble!

> *She laughs and pours another shot. Turns it around three times, blows on it, downs it.*

DAN. Look, at least have some food with that.

SARAH. We have your birthday cake.

DAN (*unenthusiastically*) Yeah… okay. I'll get some plates.

> DAN *shrugs and goes into the kitchen.*

> SARAH *quickly pours herself another shot of vodka, turns, blows and downs it. And then another… she loses count of how many times she's turned it this time, looks worried for*

*a second, then shrugs, blows and downs it again. DAN
returns with plates, a knife, forks and a beer. He plonks the
utensils down on the table and takes a long swig of beer.*

*SARAH cuts two slices of cake and hands one to DAN.
He takes a bite – SARAH watches him intensely. He looks
a bit surprised, but swallows and gives her a thumbs up.*

SARAH (*anxiously*). Do you like it?

DAN (*unsure*)....Mayonnaise?

SARAH. Because they didn't have the Miracle Whip.

DAN takes another small bite.

DAN. Actually it kind of works. I mean it's weird but it's not...
un-tasty.

SARAH beams.

SARAH. Thank you. It's your turn.

DAN takes a big swig of beer and then rolls.

Sports.

DAN. Hit me.

She punches him hard in the stomach. He doubles up.

Ow... Fuck, ow...

SARAH. You said –

DAN. I know... I meant it... shit... figuratively.

SARAH. Sorry.

DAN. No, it's okay. I think some cake just shot up my nose...
Go on.

SARAH. Which Brazilian footballer joined the New York
Cosmos in 1975?

DAN. Pele.

SARAH (*checks back of card*). Correct.

*DAN makes a triumphant face and pounds the air with
his fist.*

DAN. Yesssss.

> SARAH *stares at him in horror.*

> What's the matter?

SARAH. What did you do that for?

DAN. What?

SARAH. Yesssss.

> *She mimics his triumphant gesture, mutating it so that it looks more like an aggressive haka face.*

DAN. I wasn't doing that. I was doing this.

> *He pulls his triumphant face again.*

> Yesssss. (*Beat.*) It's a look of… triumph.

> SARAH *still looks really confused.*

> Sarah, I'm starting to feel like a complete wanker. I only got two questions right.

SARAH. It's like this game we played at school… You make a face, and I have to guess what you're thinking… Go on, think something and I'll guess it.

DAN. Okay.

> SARAH *leans in quite close to* DAN *and peers at his face for a while.* DAN *goes through a series of expressions.*

SARAH. You're sad.

DAN. I'm angry.

SARAH. You're happy.

DAN. I'm surprised.

SARAH. Oh. Do another one. (*Beat.*) You're in pain!

DAN. No, that's – I'm just thinking about what face to do.

SARAH. Oh.

> DAN *forces a grin.*

DAN. What's this one?

Pause. SARAH *drops her eye contact.*

SARAH. I don't know. I don't know why I brought it up.
I always sucked at it.

DAN. No it's me. I'm rubbish at this. You do one, go on.

SARAH *thinks about this and then slowly lifts her face and
pulls an exaggerated smile.*

You're happy.

SARAH. Yes but guess what I'm thinking about.

DAN. One Direction? Bears?

SARAH. I'm thinking I'd like a beer.

DAN. Really? After that vodka? Is that [wise] –

SARAH. I'm twenty-five.

DAN (*shrugging*). Fine.

SARAH. And get one for yourself.

DAN. Good idea.

DAN *necks the rest of his bottle and goes out to the kitchen
for more supplies. After a moment* SARAH *tentatively
touches the arm of the sofa… then the top of the table… then
the cool smoothness of the Trivial Pursuit board. Her touch
becomes more of a stroke as she takes in the textures of the
things around her. Cautiously, she places her leg on the bare
wooden floor, beyond the safety of the rug on which she
always stays. She puts her other leg down. She rolls her
limbs on the floor, feeling the wood against her skin. After
a moment she slides down and stretches out completely, like
a starfish. Her open body language is completely different to
previous scenes and we can tell that she's more than a bit
tipsy. She closes her eyes.*

DAN *enters with the beers and watches her for a moment.*
SARAH *opens her eyes.*

I'm not blind to your methods, cheater.

SARAH. What?

DAN. Getting me drunk in order to win at a board game.

SARAH ignores this comment but sits up, taking the beer from DAN. He sits down on the floor next to her.

SARAH. Guess what I'm thinking about now.

She looks really sad and lost. DAN is moved and takes a while to answer.

DAN. I don't know. You look... I don't know.

SARAH. I'm thinking about the noise of cars when they go under a bridge and it burns up my ears.

Pause.

What am I thinking about now?

Her face cracks into a huge, warm smile and her eyes sparkle mischievously.

DAN. You're happy.

SARAH. I'm thinking about you. (*Beat.*) What about now?

DAN. I don't know.

SARAH (*softly*). I'm thinking about touching your arm.

Very slowly, she reaches her hand towards his arm. They both look at it for a moment...

DAN. Sarah –

The tension builds as she leans in, closer and closer... and then prods him with a finger and makes a honking noise. There is a moment of surprise as they look at one another. Then they both laugh for a moment. The laughter suddenly dies.

SARAH. What am I thinking about now?

DAN. I don't know.

She turns his hand over and puts her palm to his. DAN allows her to do it, but he is passive.

SARAH. What am I thinking about now?

SARAH raises his hand to her lips and kisses his palm. Then she gently places it on her breast.

DAN. Sarah – don't –

*He pulls his hand back. They stare at one another. Then
SARAH leans forward, takes his face in her hands and
kisses him. He doesn't respond at first. Then we see him kiss
her back as the lights go down.*

End of Scene Five.

Scene Six

*The next afternoon. KATE, SARAH and DAN are having
a picnic in the park. KATE is making an effort to be upbeat,
DAN and SARAH are subdued and hungover. SARAH wears
sunglasses. KATE is taking birthday candles off a cake and
cutting it into slices.*

KATE. I love English weather when it's like this. It makes me
think of scones and cricket matches and Virginia Woolf and
just happy things.

DAN. Virginia Woolf wasn't 'a happy thing'. She drowned
herself.

KATE. No, I know, but you know what I mean.

DAN. Not really.

KATE. I'm just… feeling good today, okay? And I want to…
share the love. Here you go, birthday boy.

She hands DAN a slice of cake.

SARAH. His birthday was yesterday.

KATE. I know but we're celebrating today. (*Re: cake.*) How is it?

DAN. Great.

KATE. Lemon.

DAN. My favourite.

SARAH makes a scoffing noise, KATE doesn't notice.

KATE. Here, Sarah, have some.

SARAH. Hello? It's yellow.

KATE. Oh yes, sorry – I wasn't – I brought you cookies.

She starts rifling through the picnic hamper.

SARAH. I'm not hungry.

KATE. Come on, don't be grumpy. We're having a party.

SARAH. We already had a party. Last night. On his actual birthday. (*Dramatically.*) That's why I'm SO hungover.

KATE. You were drinking?

KATE *shoots a questioning look at* DAN, *who looks away, guiltily.*

SARAH (*antagonistically*). It's A Free Country.

KATE *hesitates, but chooses not to take* SARAH *on.*

KATE (*brightly*). I saw the Trivial Pursuit board was out. (*To* DAN.) How long did it take her to win?

SARAH. I didn't win. We didn't finish the game.

KATE. How come?

SARAH. We went to bed –

DAN *darts a look at* SARAH.

DAN. – because it was late when we started it and we were tired.

KATE. Well, you had a lucky escape then. She beat me in twenty minutes once. She's got an incredible memory.

She affectionately starts to put her arm around SARAH, *who remains rigid and uncomfortable, and then takes it away again, covering her disappointment.*

So... Look, I know I've been... unravelling a bit, and that's been hard on both of you. And I'm sorry for running out on you yesterday... (*To* DAN.) Especially for standing you up... That was... selfish.

DAN (*slightly flat*). You're here now.

KATE. Exactly.

She smiles at him and pecks him on the lips. SARAH *makes a 'barf' noise,* KATE *ignores her.*

So I have some news... I had a long talk with Jen last night – and I think we've come up with something. She's starting a science journal and she wants me to edit it.

DAN. A science journal?

KATE. Yeah with an emphasis on immunology.

DAN. You don't want to be in the lab any more?

KATE. Well, I think this will... I'll have to keep across all the new research. And Jen – she thinks I'll be good at it.

KATE *pulls a bottle of wine out of a shopping bag. And rummages around for a corkscrew.*

Plus I can mostly do it from home. (*Beat.*) Well, this is an auspicious start – I don't seem to have brought a corkscrew.

She looks around.

Let me go ask those guys.

KATE *exits with the bottle, leaving* DAN *and* SARAH *alone.* SARAH *takes off her sunglasses.*

SARAH (*flirtatiously*). Hey, Dan. Guess what I'm thinking about?

DAN (*uncomfortable*). I don't know.

SARAH. Last night.

DAN. Sarah, you remember what we talked about? It's really important that we don't tell Kate, okay? It would really upset her... Sarah?

SARAH. On Thursday I watched a programme about pigs. They're very intelligent. They're third in intelligence after humans and primates. And they're about tied in intelligence with dolphins. They can play computer games.

DAN. Sarah –

SARAH. They moved the joystick with their snouts. They like to dance too. One was called Steve. He really likes U2. If I were an animal, I'd be a pig. What would you be?

DAN. I don't know.

SARAH. I think you're like a frog.

DAN. Thanks.

SARAH. You're welcome.

DAN. That was sarcasm.

SARAH. Oh. No. I mean it's not a bad thing – you're not green or damp but sometimes you can be quite bouncy and then sometimes you can be really still. Hardly moving. I think maybe you're asleep, except you have your eyes open and you're just thinking things. You don't smell like one though.

DAN. You've smelled a frog?

SARAH. Once. In Virginia. We went on a picnic and it jumped into my potato salad.

DAN. What did it smell like?

SARAH. Potato.

DAN *laughs briefly in spite of himself.*

I love you.

DAN. No you don't.

SARAH. I do. When you held me last night, I realised it. And I realised that you love me too.

DAN. Sarah... I'm not sure you really understand...

SARAH. What?

DAN. What is meant by love.

SARAH (*deeply hurt*). What?

DAN. I don't love you – like *that*... You're my sister.

SARAH. Do people in England do that with their sisters?

DAN (*firmly*). Sarah. Don't. Don't mistake it for what it wasn't. We were drunk. That's all. And people are going to get very hurt. So, please, let's just forget it happened, okay?

SARAH. Keeping secrets is the same as lying.

DAN. No it's not. It's really not. Sometimes it's the best thing you can do.

SARAH. I won't tell Kate if we can do it again.

DAN. Don't – don't blackmail me.

SARAH. Why don't you want to?

DAN. Because –

SARAH. Because of my cake?

DAN. What?

SARAH. Because it wasn't as good as Kate's?

DAN. It's got nothing to do with… Look, it would upset her, okay? And we both love her and don't want to hurt her, do we?

SARAH. Don't you feel the love between *us*?

DAN. No, Sarah. All I feel is guilt.

KATE *returns, unaware of the atmosphere.*

KATE. Success! Shall we make a toast?

KATE *hands* SARAH *a can of Coke from the hamper and then pours a glass of wine for* DAN *and for herself.* SARAH *doesn't take her eyes off* DAN.

What to…?

SARAH (*looking at* DAN). To love.

KATE (*surprised*). Good idea.

SARAH. And to honesty.

KATE. Love and honesty.

They drink. Over KATE*'s head,* DAN *and* SARAH *exchange a look of war.*

SARAH (*beat*). Last night –

DAN. Kate, I was thinking, my cousin, Alice, is looking for a flatmate. She's Sarah's age – really sweet girl. I thought we could swing past on the way home, take a look.

SARAH (*shocked*). I want to keep living with you.

KATE. I don't know, Dan, with the lawyer's fees and my salary gone…

DAN. We can make it work.

SARAH. I just got here five months ago. It's not a good idea to move people with Asperger's. They can become stressed and that can make them very angry.

KATE. I guess we'll need to think about it at some point, though.

SARAH. No. I don't want to go.

SARAH *starts to tug at her hair.*

KATE (*sympathetically*). It's okay, darling. Dan's only got your best interests at heart.

SARAH. Why are you siding with him?

KATE. I'm not.

SARAH. So you're going to just dump me somewhere again? You really hate me, don't you?

KATE. No, I love you, and I have never dumped –

SARAH. I think what you feel for me is guilt not love.

KATE (*vehemently*). You know you're the most important person in the world to me.

SARAH. More important than Dan?

KATE. Sarah, stop it.

SARAH. We just toasted honesty. So be honest. Do you love me or Dan more?

KATE. Please.

SARAH. DO YOU LOVE ME OR DAN MORE?

KATE. That's an impossible question!

SARAH. Maybe Dan can help you out. Because he really *understands* love –

DAN. Sarah –

SARAH. – that's the thing with you and me, Kate. We don't really Get It. We can't feel things like other people.

KATE. What do you mean?

SARAH. Who abandons their kid sister in a place they hate? –

KATE. You were happy there –

SARAH. – no one *normal*. No one who could *empathise*.

KATE. What would you have had me do exactly? I was nineteen. I was on my own. I was grieving.

SARAH (*sarcastically*). Grieving…? Oh, wait, is that the one where you lie on the floor all day and you feel like your throat's closing up because it doesn't want to take in the air any more and you can't open your eyes because you know if you do you're going to see that gross bedspread with the green mice that Mom liked, and then you'll remember that she's dead now and that your sister put you in some *Sesame Street* hellhole with 'mentors' and 'happy spaces' and stupid, crazy kids who can't even talk and all you want is to die. No, I wouldn't know anything about *grieving*.

KATE (*quietly*). I didn't put you there.

SARAH. Sure. Right. It was welfare or something. Keep Passing The Bu–

KATE. You were already on the list.

SARAH. What?

KATE. You were on the wait list before Mom's accident, you got moved up when –

SARAH. You tried to send me away before she even died?

KATE. No… Not *me*.

SARAH (*beat*). No.

KATE. She thought it would be better for you, socially. After Dad went… you were so…

SARAH. What?

KATE. …violent. The tantrums…

SARAH. I don't believe you. Mom wouldn't do that!

KATE. She just couldn't handle… But she loved you. So much, Sarah. She only ever wanted the best for you. We both did…

SARAH *starts to hyperventilate slightly. She rolls up into a ball on the ground.*

Sarah – Sarah – it's okay. Do you want me to push on your chest?

SARAH. No!

SARAH *unfolds herself and gets up, awkwardly. Calming her breathing.*

No… I'm going to the restroom.

SARAH *puts on her sunglasses and starts to go.*

KATE. There's a café, I'll go with you.

SARAH. No! Leave me alone!

SARAH *hurries off.*

Pause.

KATE. Oh god. What did I just do?

End of Scene Six.

Scene Seven

Waiting area of a police station. Night. KATE sits on a plastic chair. Her eyes are red. DAN comes in with two cups of chalky vending-machine tea and hands one to KATE.

KATE. What did they say?

DAN. She's still in the interview room.

KATE. I don't understand. Why can't we see her? She's definitely not physically hurt?

DAN. No.

KATE. And they couldn't say whether she meant to…

DAN. No.

KATE. Exactly how far over the railings was she? Maybe she was trying to get a better look at the road.

DAN. Let's not keep going through this.

She starts to cry. DAN can't bring himself to comfort her.

Kate –

KATE. Why couldn't I keep my mouth shut?

DAN. You were provoked. She overreacted.

KATE. I made her feel like Mom didn't want her! I should have protected her.

DAN. She's not as helpless as you think she is.

KATE. She's just a child.

DAN. She's twenty-five.

KATE. With the maturity of a child.

DAN. I don't think so.

KATE. What do you mean?

DAN. I mean she – she can be – she's manipulative.

KATE. What do you mean?

DAN (*beat*). Nothing.

A POLICEWOMAN *enters and addresses* KATE.

POLICEWOMAN. Your sister would like to see you now.

KATE. Thank god.

KATE *and* DAN *make for the door.*

POLICEWOMAN (*to* DAN). Not you, sir. Just your wife.

KATE. It's alright. He and Sarah are close. I'd like him with me.

POLICEWOMAN. I'm sorry, madam. We need a word with your husband.

KATE. What? Why?

The colour drains from DAN's *face.*

DAN. Yeah, why?

End of Scene Seven.

Scene Eight

Early morning the following day. The waiting area of the police station. DAN *is slumped on a plastic chair, now wearing grey tracksuit bottoms and a white sweatshirt. He looks exhausted and grim.*

KATE *enters and stops.* DAN *raises his head.* KATE *is on automatic at the beginning of this scene, trying to make sense of what's happening.*

KATE. Where are your clothes?

DAN. They took them... for... for evidence or something.

Pause.

KATE. Did you have to sleep in a cell?

DAN. Yeah.

KATE. Fuck.

DAN. How's Sarah?

KATE. Wiped out. She had to go through some tests. They were pretty awful.

DAN. They said you'd gone.

KATE. They took us to a… specialist unit – 'The Haven'. I kind of hoped it'd turn out to be a spa. It didn't. (*Beat.*) What happens now?

DAN. I've been released on bail… I'll stay at Tom's tonight.

KATE (*beat*). Okay.

Pause.

DAN. What about you?

KATE. I need to pick up the house keys. They had to… they wanted to… look around. (*Beat.*) They took our mattress.

KATE starts to cry. After a moment of deliberation DAN gets up and goes to her. He puts his arms around her and she sinks into him. They hold the embrace for a long time.

DAN. I'm so sorry you have to go through this. I'm so, so sorry. I love you. So much.

KATE. I love you.

She starts crying again, he strokes her hair. Then she pulls away, blows her nose.

DAN. They won't let me see her, so when you get home, let me know and I'll come over, have a word with her.

Pause.

KATE. That's breaking the conditions of your bail, isn't it?

DAN. They won't know.

KATE. No. It's not a good idea.

DAN. What do you mean?

KATE. She's too upset. She's traumatised.

DAN. We're all fucking traumatised. That's the point. Let's get her to drop the charges and the nightmare's over.

KATE. No.

DAN. Kate!

KATE. She tried to kill herself.

DAN. And you think that's my fault?

KATE. I don't care whose fault it is. I just want her to be okay.

DAN. My god! You think I did it. You think I raped your sister.

KATE (*beat; quietly*). The police think there's a case against you, they think –

DAN. Who gives a fuck. What do you think?!

KATE. I don't know.

DAN. JESUS! FUCK!

He stands up and kicks a chair. Then he slumps on to the floor, his head in his hands.

KATE watches him, torn, and then joins him on the floor, pulling his head into her lap. She holds him for a while, stroking him, then she gently eases away from him.

KATE. Dan, I need you to tell me, did something happen last night? Between you?

DAN can't look at her.

Please. Look me in the eye and tell me nothing happened.

DAN wipes his eyes.

DAN. We kissed.

KATE. Oh god.

DAN. And we shared a bed. But fully clothed. That was it.

I swear.

KATE. Oh god.

She scrambles to her feet.

I need – I need…

She collapses into a chair.

DAN. That's all. I promise.

Pause.

Are you okay?

KATE. I thought I was going to be sick.

DAN. I'll get someone.

KATE. Don't. I'm all right. I'm fine.

Pause.

How could you do that? Ply her with alcohol? Take advantage of her?

DAN. *She* seduced *me*.

KATE. What?

DAN. She thinks she's in love with me.

KATE. None of this is making any sense.

DAN. Listen, the whole rape-victim thing is an act. You've got to get her to say what really happened.

KATE. What really happened? What really happened is that you did something to her that made her so unhappy she tried to dash her brains out by jumping sixty feet on to a dual carriageway. (*Beat.*) Now, what was that, Dan?

End of Scene Eight.

Scene Nine

Six weeks later, early evening. KATE *and* DAN *sit across a table from each other in an East London hipster bar. They're nervous.* DAN *looks around.*

DAN. Interesting place.

KATE. Yeah. I think it's just opened. It's supposed to be an 'artisanal watering hole'. Whatever that is. Anyway I thought, you know, why not.

DAN (*beat*). You look…

Embarrassed, KATE *quickly covers up her forehead with her hand.*

KATE. Oh I know… My eyebrows.

DAN. What?

KATE. There was this woman in the mall… An 'Eyebrow Architect'. Jen said it would make me look younger but I think I just look surprised… Which I pretty much am every time I look in the mirror.

DAN. No, I just was going to say you look good.

KATE. Oh. (*Beat.*) Thanks.

Pause.

How's work?

DAN. Difficult. I may not be there much longer. (*Beat.*) They know.

KATE (*shocked*). How?

DAN. I assumed you told them.

KATE. Me? No! Why would I?

DAN. Then how?

KATE. Dan, I swear. I wouldn't.

DAN. Sarah?

KATE. No! She wouldn't either.

DAN. How do you know?

KATE. She's not vindictive like that.

DAN scoffs.

People talk.

DAN (*bitterly*). Yeah. People.

A WAITRESS appears. She's a hipster, but perky.

WAITRESS. Hi, guys! Did you have a chance to look at the Feelin' Thirsty list?

DAN (*simultaneous*). Oh… no.

KATE (*simultaneous*). Sorry…

WAITRESS. No problem. Would you like me to run you through the Daily IceBreakers?

KATE. What?

WAITRESS. The specials.

KATE. Oh, yeah. Sure.

WAITRESS. Perfect! Well, firstly we're excited to inform you that our glassware is kept chilled to exactly minus thirty degrees so our drinks are maintained at the perfect temperature. All of our ice is chosen by Morten Gunardsson, our ice chef, from a twice frozen block of spring water sourced in Norway. First up we have 'Call me Walter', which is what we call a 'palate fluffer' combining peach schnapps –

DAN. Sorry, can I just have a beer?

KATE. Yeah me too?

WAITRESS (*annoyed*). Two beers. Right.

She smiles insincerely and leaves.

KATE. I think we just ruined her night.

DAN. Yeah, she's probably relating the terrible news to Morten right now.

KATE. He could burst out of that kitchen with his ice pick any minute.

They grin at each other, enjoying the joke. KATE *inches her hand across the table towards him.* DAN *inches his hand forward and they touch fingertips. They look at one another for a moment. Then* DAN *withdraws.*

DAN. I can't do this.

KATE. This bar? I know, it's awful, isn't it? –

DAN. No… this – this… when I don't know when you're…

KATE (*beat*). I haven't decided.

DAN. You haven't decided.

KATE. I need – to think.

DAN. You've had six weeks to think. I need to know where we stand.

KATE. I can't give you an answer yet.

DAN. Why not? The case has been dropped.

KATE (*quietly*). She doesn't lie.

DAN. Rubbish! There is no evidence. There is no case.

KATE. Sarah –

DAN. Fuck Sarah! Do you love me or not?

KATE. I love you.

DAN. But you believe her over me.

KATE (*cornered*). Look, all I know is that she needs me. She's depressed.

DAN. I'm depressed. I need you.

KATE. Not like she does.

DAN. Kate, please. (*Beat.*) We will organise somewhere for Sarah to live. You can see her every day. You can help her plot the defamation of every man in the Northern Hemisphere if you want, but please come back to me. I miss you.

KATE. I miss you too.

DAN. Come back then.

KATE (*beat*). I want to but… we can't just pick up where we left off.

DAN. Okay. (*Beat.*) We could go somewhere? Abroad?

KATE (*unsure*). Like a holiday?

DAN. If you like… Somewhere hot… Somewhere cold… I don't mind.

KATE (*beat*). When?

DAN. Soon…?

KATE. Yeah – okay – maybe…

DAN. Okay!

KATE. Is this crazy?!

DAN. This is the sanest thing we've done in months.

They grin at each other. KATE *scrambles around in her bag for her diary.*

KATE. Let me just check Sarah's dates. We've only just found a college – I don't want to yank her out…

DAN. Why would you 'yank her out'?

KATE. Well, if she's making friends, I don't –

DAN (*incredulously*). You're not going to bring her?

KATE. Look… I really think… if we all started again –

DAN. Have you lost your mind?

KATE. I'm all she has. I can't just leave her.

DAN (*beat*). Wow. She's got you right where she wants you, hasn't she?

KATE. What's that supposed to mean?

DAN (*fiercely*). She's going to make sure you miss any shot at happiness.

KATE. Dan – please, don't.

DAN. You've got to get it into your head, Kate, she's not a child. She's a grown woman. A manipulative grown woman.

KATE. She has Asperger's! –

DAN. That's got nothing to do with it.

KATE. You know it's very convenient – your vacillating perception of Sarah's capabilities. I remember you being very concerned about her helplessness when you persuaded me to give up my career.

DAN. She wants you miserable.

KATE. She shouldn't bother, you've done a great job of it yourself.

DAN. She's plotted this whole thing to split us up.

KATE. Is your ego really so stellar that you need not just me, but my sister, to be head over heels in love with you?

DAN. Oh no, this isn't about me. That is something I'm very clear on now. This is about you.

KATE. Me?

DAN. It's not my blood she wants. It's yours. I'm just the worm on the hook.

KATE. No.

DAN. She's exacting this brilliant revenge for you leaving her all those years ago. We both heard her views.

KATE. NO! Don't put this back on me again. Don't you – don't you do that –

KATE *tries to contain tears of anger.*

What she did – the, Jesus… the… suicide attempt –

DAN. Alleged –

KATE. – was because of her feelings for you – not –

The WAITRESS *reappears with their beers.*

WAITRESS. Two beers, guys. Can I interest you in any of our bar snacks? Today's specials are honey-glazed mini chorizo nestled on a bed of heritage –

KATE. No, no, we don't want anything. Just… can you leave us alone for five minutes?

The WAITRESS *gives* KATE *a 'sorry I exist' look and humphs off.*

DAN. Kate, please. I'm not trying to hurt you. I love you. I'm just trying to help you see the facts.

KATE. You're right. I *should* just look at the facts.

She stands up.

And here they are: my sister tried to kill herself, and she doesn't lie. You do lie, *and* you were prepared to let me carry the guilt.

DAN. I told you what happened.

KATE. You told me a version of it. Because you got caught.

DAN. You're really going to walk away from our whole marriage because of one drunken kiss?

KATE. Watch me.

KATE *goes, leaving* DAN *alone.*

End of Scene Nine.

Scene Ten

*Nine months later. 8 p.m. KATE and SARAH are wrapped up
in coats and scarves, standing outside a cinema. They're in
good spirits. SARAH looks much younger than we've seen her
looking before. Her hair is in a ponytail and she's rummaging
through a backpack with a clip-on stuffed sock monkey dangling
from it.*

KATE. I enjoyed that.

SARAH. I liked the songs, but of course it was extremely
inaccurate. There's no way they could have travelled all that
way in two days because everyone knows that Beluga
whales can't swim faster then about five miles an hour, so
it's just not realistic.

KATE. Kind of not realistic that they were talking either, right?
Are there any Maltesers left?

SARAH. No, I left them under the seat. Actually they do talk.
They can click and whistle and even squawk. I doubt they
sound like Tom Hanks though. Can we go to a movie next
weekend? I want to see *Ghost Park*.

KATE. Yikes. I may have to hide behind you. Have you found
your Oyster card yet? I'm freezing my ass off here.

SARAH. I thought it was in my calculator pouch, but I can't
see it.

KATE. Check your coat pockets. Here, I'll take your bag.

*SARAH hands her bag to KATE and digs around in her
pockets. As she does so, she doesn't notice a scrunched-up
empty Maltesers bag fall out. KATE stares at it.*

Sarah. What's that?

SARAH looks at the bag.

SARAH. A Maltesers bag.

KATE. You said you left them under the seat.

SARAH. Actually I ate them all, so I put the bag in my pocket.

KATE. You lied.

SARAH. Sorry.

KATE. But you lied.

> SARAH *looks blank.*

I thought you – you've never lied…

SARAH. Oh yeah, I lie about lots of stuff. I can do that now.
Cool, huh?

> *End of Scene Ten.*

Scene Eleven

*Two days later. Late afternoon. A cafe. DAN sits at a table. He
wears casual clothes and plays nervously with the sugar sachets.*

*SARAH enters and spots DAN. She is wearing trendy student
stuff – jeans, a little T-shirt, colourful jewellery. She carries a
tray with two cans of Coke.*

SARAH. Hi.

DAN. Hi.

> SARAH *sits.*

SARAH. I got you a Coke.

DAN (*indicating the red cans of Coke*). Is it a Special Day
today then?

SARAH. I don't do that any more. It was becoming a
Psychological Crutch.

> SARAH *turns the can three times, blows on it and then
> opens it.*

I come here on the bus sometimes. It's only two stops from
college. There are four bus routes, which I take by myself.
And I get a student discount – look.

> *She shows him her student card.*

Guess what, I've been there nearly three whole terms now.
For Real! It's quite hard but I like it. And I have three
friends: Melanie, Leila and Omar. But Melanie says that
Omar *likes* me likes me so I'm going to Let Him Down
Gently. I like him but only as a friend because I'm Involved
With Someone Else at the moment.

DAN (*drily*). Lucky him.

SARAH. When I finish the course, I get a diploma, which means
I can get a job with animals in a zoo or maybe I'll work in
a rescue sanctuary. Or I might volunteer my Skillset to the
American Bears' club. They've made me an Honorary Grizzly.

DAN. Sarah, why am I here?

SARAH. Because I asked you to come.

DAN. Yes, I know. Why did you ask?

SARAH (*carefully*). Because I... (*Beat.*) Because I wanted to
say sorry... about what I said. In the police station. When
they asked me the question I told a lie. I knew the answer but
I said something else.

Pause.

DAN (*shocked*). Have you told Kate?

SARAH. Yes.

DAN. When? When did she find out?

SARAH. Monday at 8.07 p.m.

DAN. What did she say?

SARAH. She was very mad and then she cried. For a long time.
It was really bad.

DAN *stares at the table, his mind whirring.*

DAN. Why did you do it?

SARAH. It seemed like they wanted me to say it.

DAN. Who?

SARAH. The policewoman and the nurse. They asked me stuff
and I said yes.

DAN. You said yes because they asked you?!

SARAH (*beat*). Maybe also because I was angry and sad with everything.

DAN. Sarah, you destroyed our marriage.

SARAH. Sorry.

DAN (*bitterly*). 'Sorry'!

Pause.

Are we done here?

SARAH. No. I wanted to say thank you too. Because that was the first time that I lied in my whole life. Which even though it was a bad thing, was a good thing too. (*Beat.*) I'll show you…

SARAH rummages in her bag and pulls out a book. She doesn't read easily, but she's read this many times and almost knows it off by heart.

It's called *Lying in Autism: A Cognitive Milestone*. Louise, my counsellor, showed it to me… (*Reading.*) 'When an autistic individual begins to lie, it can lead to additional problems, as does lying in non-autistic children. At the same time, the advent of lying behavior can be viewed as reaching a new cognitive milestone and can be seen as a reason to celebrate.' So you see, something to celebrate!

DAN. Christ. You don't have any idea what you did to me.

SARAH. The case got dropped.

DAN. That's not good enough.

SARAH. I know.

They stare at one another for a moment.

But we had fun that night, didn't we? I think we could be buddies now.

DAN starts to laugh uncontrollably.

Why are you laughing?

DAN. I don't know.

DAN *continues to laugh until he's drained*. SARAH *waits for him to finish*.

SARAH. This isn't a date, you know.

DAN. What?

SARAH. In case you thought it was… Sorry. But you're not really My Type. (*Beat*.) I'm not really Your Type either, am I?

DAN. No.

KATE *appears at the door of the café*. DAN *stares at her as if she's a mirage*.

SARAH. I have to go now. Bye. Good luck with everything.

She joins KATE *at the door*.

KATE. Why don't you wait in the car for me?

SARAH. Okay.

SARAH *takes the car keys from* KATE *and exits*. KATE *and* DAN *stare at each other*. KATE *slowly approaches the table*.

DAN. She didn't say you were coming.

KATE. I asked her not to.

DAN. Why?

KATE. I was afraid you wouldn't want to see me.

Pause.

How are you?

DAN. Okay.

She sits at the table.

Pause.

KATE. You look skinny.

DAN. Yeah… It's amazing what a few rounds with a tropical parasite will do.

KATE. Did you have fun?… Apart from the parasites I mean?

DAN. I climbed some volcanoes, smoked some weed, did some thinking… the usual 'finding yourself' shit I guess.

KATE. And did you? Find yourself?

DAN. I found a lot of other people trying to find themselves. (*Beat.*) She seems happy – Sarah.

KATE. Yes.

DAN. She said she told you.

KATE. Dan, I'm so –

DAN. Don't.

Pause.

Does it make a difference? Now you know the truth?

KATE. Of course it does.

DAN (*beat*). I've met someone.

KATE. Oh. Is it serious?

DAN. I don't know. Maybe.

KATE (*with difficulty*). I'm happy for you.

DAN. So if you want to use that for the divorce...

KATE. No –

DAN. I don't mind –

KATE. I know, but you don't have to. Thanks.

Pause.

DAN. Have you...? Met anyone?

KATE. No. Well, there was someone – but he wasn't...

DAN (*aggressively*). What?

KATE (*quietly*)....you. (*Beat.*) We're going back to the States for a bit.

DAN. Oh.

KATE. When Sarah's finished her course... We got her fund back – well, some of it.

DAN. Great.

KATE (*beat*). Dad got in touch. He wants to… 'reconnect'…

DAN. Wow.

KATE. Yeah. The redemption of the dying.

DAN. Is he?

KATE. Liver cancer. Jack Daniels won in the end.

DAN. Sorry. If that's… [appropriate]

> KATE *shifts her hand towards him across the table. It's a cautious gesture.*

KATE. I miss you.

> *He looks down at her hand but doesn't reciprocate. She withdraws her hand awkwardly.*

> I'd better go. Sarah's been wanting a car for a while – I'm not completely sure she doesn't mean mine.

> *She stands, pulls an A4 envelope out of her bag and hands it to* DAN.

> Here. They're signed.

DAN. I'll get them back to you as soon as I can.

KATE. Sure, whatever – I mean there's no rush. (*Beat.*) Give me a call if you're… if you want.

> DAN *can't look at her.*

> Okay.

> *She turns to leave.*

DAN. You were wrong you know.

> KATE *turns back.*

> No maternal instinct. She's lucky to have you.

> KATE *fights back the tears. She and* DAN *look at each other for a moment. She smiles at him as the lights fade.*

> *The End.*

Other Titles in this Series

A Nick Hern Book

Burning Bridges first published in Great Britain in 2016 as a paperback original by Nick Hern Books Limited, The Glasshouse, 49a Goldhawk Road, London W12 8QP, in association with Sally Knyvette Productions and Theatre503, London

Burning Bridges copyright © 2016 Amy Shindler

Amy Shindler has asserted her moral right to be identified as the author of this work

Cover image by Mihaela Bodlovic

Designed and typeset by Nick Hern Books, London
Printed in the UK by Mimeo Ltd, Huntingdon, Cambridgeshire PE29 6XX

A CIP catalogue record for this book is available from the British Library

ISBN   978 1 84842 594 1

www.nickhernbooks.co.uk

facebook.com/nickhernbooks

twitter.com/nickhernbooks